QUICK EXPERT'S GUIDE

Write Your Own Blog

Luisa Plaja

ROSEN
PUBLISHING®

New York

Published in 2014 by The Rosen Publishing Group, Inc.
29 East 21st Street, New York, NY 10010

Senior editor: Julia Adams
Design: Rocket Design (East Anglia) Ltd.
All images and graphic elements: Shutterstock

Library of Congress Cataloging-in-Publication Data

Plaja, Luisa, author.
Write your own blog/Luisa Plaja.—First edition.
    pages cm.—(Quick expert's guide)
Audience: Grades 5 to 7.
Includes bibliographical references and index.
ISBN 978-1-4777-2819-2 (library binding)—
ISBN 978-1-4777-2821-5 (pbk.)—
ISBN 978-1-4777-2822-2 (6-pack)
1. Blogs—Juvenile literature. I. Title.
TK5105.8884.P57 2014
006.7'52—dc23

2013018135

Manufactured in the United States of America

CPSIA Compliance Information: Batch #W14YA: For further information, contact Rosen Publishing, New York, New York, at 1-800-237-9932.

>>>CONTENTS<<<

We have highlighted blogs, Web sites and tools throughout this guide in bold; we didn't want to overload you with URLs, but you should be able to find them really easily through search engines.

THE UTTERLY EXCELLENT WORLD OF BLOGGING!

Would you like to carve out a corner of cyberspace and call it your own? Want to find people who share your interests, however obscure? Need to tell everyone you've had a bad day, and wish you could get responses from sympathetic readers all over the world? Writing a blog could be for you!

Blogs are as diverse and individual as their owners. People keep blogs that reflect their interests: music, books, crafts, films, sports, celebrities, saving the planet, saving the planet from celebrities— anything goes! Others post pictures and discuss their everyday lives in colorful, interactive online journals.

It's easy to start your own blog, and with the help of this guide, you can be an expert in no time. Get tips on linking to social networks, finding readers, dealing with comment spam and much more. Before you know it, you'll be connecting with like-minded people all over the world and wondering why you didn't start blogging sooner.

WHIP OUT THE WRITING CAP AND GET YOUR CREATIVE CHAKRAS ALIGNED FOR THE QUICK EXPERT TEAM'S SHOW-AND-TELL ON:

The man who became a **millionaire** through his blog...

...and the woman who **lost** her job through hers

How to choose an **original** name for your blog

How to avoid Internet **meanies**

The mind-boggling choice of software you have and how to know which one is the **best** one for you.

How to use social networks to **shout** about your blog

Chapter 1

STEP INTO THE BLOGOSPHERE!

✳ WHAT IS A BLOG?

Broadly speaking, a blog is any Web site that's designed to be updated regularly. The latest entry usually displays at the top of the main page, with older entries pushed down by newer ones but not deleted. There's typically a place in each entry for readers to add their own great thoughts and enthusiastic praise (or otherwise), also known as the comments section.

A blog entry is called a post. Posts can take the form of text, pictures, links to other sites or all of the above. They can also contain audio and video elements. Many blogs include pages and sidebars containing more permanent facts, such as details about the blog's author, contact information and favorite sites.

Updating a blog is simple. All you need is access to your blogging software. You can blog from any place or device that has an Internet connection.

✳ WHERE DID THE WORD "BLOG" COME FROM?

Internet historians are always arguing about issues like this, but many of them agree that the word "blog" originated in the term "Weblog," used by Jorn Barger in 1997 to describe his online records of links that he visited while surfing the Net. Most historians also accept that this term was shortened to "blog" by Peter Merholz in 1999, on his site **http://www.peterme.com**.

The word "blog" proved to be catchy, and soon people were using it as a verb as well as a noun. It's now fully absorbed into English vocabulary, and lots of related words have come from it.

There's loads more about the history of blogging at CNET: http://news.cnet.com/2100-1025_3-6168681.html

>> TECHIE TALK <<

BLOG WORDS

Blogger – A person who runs a blog (and also the name of the blogging software owned by Google).

Blogosphere – The wider community of bloggers around the globe.

Blogroll – A list of links to other blogs, usually found in a blog's sidebar.

Blogebrity – A person who achieves fame through blogging.

Audio blog – A blog featuring sound recordings.

Vlog – A blog featuring video recordings.

Moblog – A blog that's updated by mobile phone.

Splog – A blog that consists entirely of spam.

✳ HOW BIG IS THE BLOGOSPHERE?

The short answer is: it's impossible to say! New blogs are springing up all the time, while older blogs are left to gather Internet dust, or are deleted altogether. Also, the programs that count blogs might exclude certain kinds of sites, such as those marked "private" or ones that use non-Roman writing systems.

Guesses can be made about the size of the blogosphere, though. At the end of 2011, global marketing company **Nielsen** reported the tracking of 181 million public blogs worldwide. **Technorati**, a large search engine for blogs, provides detailed yearly "State of the Blogosphere" posts, and currently lists about 1.3 million blogs. The largest number of blogs in its directory are in the lifestyle category, closely followed by entertainment and then business, technology and sports.

http://blog.nielsen.com
http://technorati.com

✳ CELEBRITY BLOGGING

There are two main types of celebrity blogs: those that feature news about the entertainment industry, and ones that are actually written by famous people. The first category outnumbers the second by a large amount, and some of the world's most popular blogs are about celebrity gossip.

The categories start to overlap when people become famous for their blogging — a phenomenon also known as "blogebrity." The most well-known example of this is probably Perez Hilton, a US blogger whose gossip site gained so much notoriety that he has been invited to make guest appearances on television programs such as *Victorious* on Nickelodeon.

Many stars seem more comfortable limiting their thoughts to under 140 characters than they do posting in the blogosphere, so **Twitter** is usually the best place to look for updates from famous folk. Watch out for the blue badge with a check that marks a verified account — i.e., showing that the person using the name is the actual celebrity, or someone the celebrity has employed to tweet on his or her behalf.

Still, some celebrities do write blogs — or hire others to blog for them. They post about their opinions, show pictures of their most recent gig or tell you when their latest film or album is out. Famous bloggers include chef Jamie Oliver, rapper Tinie Tempah, singer Avril Lavigne, DJ and musician Moby, television personality Kim Kardashian and actor Wil Wheaton. Movie star Alec Baldwin is a contributor to **The Huffington Post**, a world-famous group blog.

One profession that's likely to inspire blogging is that of writing, and a lot of popular authors also run great blogs. Some examples of author blogs are those run by Neil Gaiman, Meg Cabot and Cassandra Clare. If there are authors you love, it's always worth checking online to see if they blog about their lives and their books.

Keris Stainton, journalist and author of novels for teenagers, talks about her 9th anniversary of blogging.

SAY WHAT?

" I started a personal blog nine years ago as a way to make myself write every day and as a distraction from the job I wasn't happy in. I soon got completely addicted and I've had dozens of blogs since, but I've always had a personal blog and have blogged a LOT over the past nine years.

Blogging opened up a whole new world to me and not only would I not be where I am today career-wise, I wouldn't have met most of my lovely friends. I can't even imagine... "

From http://www.dellasays.wordpress.com

✳ A selection of the world's most popular blogs

TMZ — Celebrity gossip at **http://www.TMZ.com**.

TreeHugger — Green issues at **http://www.treehugger.com**.

BoingBoing — Technology and politics at **http://www.boingboing.net**.

Perez Hilton — Hollywood gossip at **http://www.perezhilton.com**.

I Can Has Cheezburger? — Humorously captioned photos at **http://www.icanhas.cheezburger.com**.

The Sartorialist — Fashion blog at **http://www.thesartorialist.blogspot.com**.

The Offside — Soccer community blog at **http://www.theoffside.com**.

✳ Great blogs run by teenagers

Teen Granny — A blog about "knitting, baking and a puppy named Posy," written by Scarlett, a teenage girl from London. **http://teenagegranny.blogspot.com**

Ultra Culture — This film and entertainment blog was started by British teenager Charlie and is still going strong. It was declared "enjoyably snarky" by *Time Out* magazine. **http://www.ultraculture.co.uk**

Rookie Mag — This magazine aimed at teenage girls was founded by Tavi Gevinson of *Style Rookie*. The team states, "We post just three times a day — after school, after dinner, and before bed." **http://rookiemag.com**

The Mile Long Bookshelf — A book blog run by teenager Amber, whose reviews have been quoted on the covers of popular teen books. **http://www.themilelongbookshelf.com**

Filmonic — This high-ranking, popular film blog was started by a teen named Liam in 2007 and has been regularly updated ever since. **http://filmonic.com**

Bookhi — Run by teenager Zoe, this blog features book reviews, interviews with authors and guest posts by authors. **http://bookhi.blogspot.com**

✳ HOW TO FIND INTERESTING BLOGS

Go to a blog directory, such as **Technorati** or **IceRocket**, or visit the specialized blog areas of many search engines, for example **Google Blog Search**. Enter a fun search term and see what comes up, or browse through the categories and special features.

Some blogging software providers highlight particular blogs, throwing up a random mix of quirky sites to check out every day. See **Freshly Pressed** at **http://discover.wordpress.com** and **Typepad's Showcase — http://www.typepad.com/showcase**. Also take a look at blog discovery sites like **http://www.stumbleupon.com**.

The friends you follow on social networks like **Facebook** and **Twitter** will often link to great blogs. Some people also post links to pages hosted by aggregators — sites that collect links about similar topics and group them together. An example is **http://paper.li,** which displays links in a format that looks a bit like a newspaper page.

http://www.google.com/blogsearch

Think about what entertains you (music, cooking, reading, photography, film) and use one of the methods above to find a recently updated blog on the subject. Then follow the links in the blogroll to find three more interesting sites. See if any of these lead to even more great sites, and so on. Bookmark the ones you'd like to visit again and make some notes about what drew you to them in the first place, and what kept you reading and wanting to return. These notes and links will come in handy when creating your own blog.

DIY DUDE

Find some blogs that inspire you

Dude!

❋ GREAT REASONS TO START A BLOG

Lots of people write blogs. Why should you join them?

Do you want to keep track of what you've been up to? You could log the books you've read, baseball games you've been to, game levels you've conquered, clothes you've made or pictures you've taken. A blog can give you a personal online scrapbook that you can refer to at any time.

Have you ever wondered whether anyone else has the same interests as you, however unusual these are? Try blogging about them and watch as people from the other side of the world find you and match your eclectic knowledge, perhaps even adding to it, if that's possible...

Or maybe you're not looking for a huge audience, but you'd just like a place where you can stay in touch with old friends and faraway family members and tell them about what's going on in your life. A blog is a great place to do this, and you can make it viewable only to people you have invited. In fact, if you want to restrict who has access to your innermost thoughts, you can set a blog to be fully private. Blogs can be a great way to vent stress and relax, as they allow you to let off steam through your writing.

Whatever your preferences, blogging can give you a creative outlet. It's a piece of Internet space that you can build, personalize and be proud of.

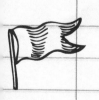

> ❝ It wasn't until I found the world of book blogging that I discovered people who got me... I've found people who love books from all over the world. ❞
>
> **Jess from Jess Hearts Books**
> http://jessheartsbooks.blogspot.com

SAY WHAT?

✳ CREATIVE BLOGGING IDEAS

✳ What's your blogging style?

Not completely sure what you'd like to blog about? Here are some blogging styles to inspire you.

Mastermind. What's your specialist subject? Perhaps you're the go-to person for the latest sports news. Or you might be a whiz at decorating unusual birthday cakes, or a total film buff with a passion for obscure, subtitled films. Maybe you know the characters from a certain soap or reality show inside out, and you're always amusing your friends with predictions about what will happen next. Or perhaps vintage cars are your thing, or you love taking pictures of rare wildlife. Whatever you're into, someone out in the blogosphere will share your interests.

Not-so-secret diarist. Do you like sharing details of your life with people? Some people enjoy keeping a general online journal, talking about their day and discussing their likes and dislikes.

Mystery blogger. Would you rather steer well away from the personal? Some people adopt an online personality under an invented name, or even blog from the point of view of totally fictional characters.

brainiac

secret identity

blah blah blahhh...

Advice columnist!

Columnist. Do you have strong feelings about politics and social issues? Would you like to discuss them with others? Focus your blog on something you care deeply about. You don't have to be an absolute expert in the subject you feature — in fact, blogging can be a good way to find out more.

Project leader. Would you prefer a more short-term blog, such as a travel diary of your summer vacation? Giving yourself a fixed amount of time for blogging or a specific theme such as "A Year in the Life of..." or "30 Holiday Photographs by..." can help to keep you focused.

Advice columnist. Can you help others — or ask for help yourself? Your blog will be truly interactive if you ask readers for advice, as well as inviting them to send you their questions or problems that you can answer in future posts. For example, you could start a movie recommending service or give advice on fashion and accessories.

Undecided. Still not quite sure yet? You might change your mind about the focus of your blog over time, and that's fine! It's great to be flexible.

✳ HOW DO BLOGGERS MAKE MONEY FROM BLOGGING?

You might have heard of professional bloggers, or people who make a living exclusively from blogging. Some of these are employed by large companies to maintain journals about certain products or services, and others are freelance journalists who sell their expertise and articles to popular sites.

There are also ways that nonexpert bloggers can earn money through their sites. Some bloggers make and sell craft items, for example, linking their blogs to an online shop. Or if a blog becomes very popular, it might attract advertisers who will pay to place links and images on the site, or offer to sponsor posts about a promotional topic. Site owners usually need to build their reputation first, and prove that they have a large number of followers and viewers.

Bloggers over age 18 can sign up for services like **Google AdSense**, which send a stream of advertising that's related to the topics on their site. There are also affiliate programs that people can join. These offer bloggers money in exchange for sending customers and sales their way. An example of an affiliate program is **Amazon Associates**, where bloggers get a small percentage of any sale made after a buyer has clicked a special link on their site.

Another way some bloggers make money is by asking for it directly! They display "donate" buttons or "tip jars" on their blogs, giving readers a link to a site where they can make a donation.

✳ Review blogs

Some companies are happy to send products to be reviewed on successful blogs with loyal audiences. There are bloggers who receive skin care products, books, clothes, tickets for shows and so on. If you build up your site and reputation — and remember to include contact details on your blog — you might find yourself getting some offers!

✳ Caution!

If you're approached by an advertiser or someone offering you free goods, always get full permission from your parents before accepting. Note that many programs require you to be over 18. Never give out personal information, phone numbers or bank account details.

REALITY CHECK

OFFICIAL REALITY CHECKER

THIS CARD CERTIFIES THAT
_ _ _ _ Melvin _ _ _ _
IS OFFICIALLY APPOINTED
TO CHECK REALITY ON
BEHALF OF THE QUICK
EXPERT'S GUIDE

APPROVED

☑ Successful blogging ideas

You may have heard of Alex Tew, the man who became a millionaire when he sold space on his Web site to advertisers pixel by pixel – and blogged about it. Alex Tew's blog is no longer updated but is still available to read at http://www.milliondollarhomepage.com/blog.php.

There have been other blogging successes, such as the woman who sold a book based on her blog **The Julie/Julia Project**, where she challenged herself to cook every recipe from a classic cookbook by Julia Child in the course of a year. The book, *Julie & Julia*, was later made into a film starring Meryl Streep. You can still read the original blog at http://juliepowellbooks.com.

New Albany is an example of a fictional blog—or is it? Make up your own mind as you follow the adventures of 16-year-old Becca Stardust, starting in the archives to get the full story. http://beccastardust.tumblr.com/archive

There are lots of other interesting and inspiring stories online. The Young Bloggers section on a site called Retire at 21 gives a list of award-winning and money-making young bloggers, many of whom are teenagers.

http://www.retireat21.com

OFFICIAL FORM C-185A

>> TECHIE TALK <<

WEB SITE, BLOG, MICRO-BLOG, SOCIAL NETWORK — WHAT'S THE DIFFERENCE?

A **Web site** is a collection of pages on the Web, usually featuring links and information.

A **blog** is a type of Web site that displays updates in reverse chronological order. Examples can be found at **WordPress** and **Blogger**.

A **microblog** is a type of blog that displays a smaller amount of information, for example, captioned photos or emoticons. Examples can be found at **Tumblr** and **Plurk**.

A **social network** is a group of interconnected people who follow each other's updates. Examples are **Facebook** and **Twitter**.

The Quick Expert team LOVES their vintage social network!

GET REAL! Bloggers talk about what inspired them to start their sites

Reuben, 13, would like to encourage others to blog:
"I like blogging because it's an easy way to keep writing, and I find it quite relaxing when I'm in a good mood. I think that the only thing I can say about blogging is to try it! It can really be invaluable when you need something to write about, or draw inspiration from. Nobody really knows until they've done it."

Zoe, 13, started blogging after browsing online:
"I started book blogging for a simple reason – I was inspired by other blogs. I love browsing the Web, and came across a blog aimed at my age. I searched through and discovered so much: recommended reads, competitions, giveaways and even more books. It looked like so much fun to run and I was definitely right."
Zoe runs Bookhi: http://bookhi.blogspot.com

QUICK EXPERT SUMMARY

- 💿 Blogs can be simple online diaries, or they can focus on a particular subject or activity.

- 💿 There are millions of blogs all over the world, covering thousands of different topics and themes.

- 💿 Blogging can help you connect with people who share your interests.

- 💿 A successful blog could mean you'll start to receive products for review, and it could possibly even lead to fame!

- Blogging is easy, rewarding and fun.

Chapter 2

GETTING STARTED

You've looked at some interesting blogs and been inspired to start your own. You have an idea of a theme, or what you'd like to blog about, even if it's simply "my life." Congratulations! You're nearly ready to create your blog. But first there are a few decisions to make.

✳ A BLOG BY ANY OTHER NAME...

When it comes to choosing a name for your blog, take your time. Try brainstorming for a while, jotting down every idea that comes into your head. If you've decided on a theme for your blog, focus on that as you write. Blog names that are obviously connected to the themes of a site will help interested readers know at a glance that they've found the right place.

Now have a look at your list. Does anything there sound vaguely familiar? Check a search engine to find out whether a site with that name already exists. Go for originality if at all possible.

Nothing unique on your list? Maybe you can combine a couple of your ideas and make up a word of your own. Invented words can be eye-catching and intriguing. Also, shorter blog names can be easier to remember. An example is **Gizmodo**, a popular technology blog.

If you prefer a longer name, then check that the initials make a good acronym — one that doesn't spell anything you'd rather it didn't! Or think about a nickname for your site.

Still stuck? Try a creative name generator, such as **Wordoid**, which will give suggestions including the word of your choice. For example, entering "Rosen" gives the suggestions "Rosenteen" and "Rosentially," both currently available as Web addresses.

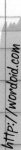

http://wordoid.com

✳ TAGLINES

As well as a title, you can choose a tagline, which is a kind of subheading that gives more information or a message about your site's content. This can be particularly useful if you've settled on a name that doesn't relate specifically to your content. It can also be fun and attractive to readers. For example, **The Teen Diaries** blog has the tagline "The Ultimate Life Guide for Young, Urban Women." **Teen Granny's** is "Knitting, Baking and a Puppy Named Posy."

✳ WHICH BLOGGING SOFTWARE WILL YOU USE?

The most popular blogging platforms include **Blogger**, **WordPress**, **Xanga**, **Tumblr** and **Posterous**. Most of these are free to use and provide templates so that you can easily customize your blog and publish posts with next to no technical knowledge. If you know how to send an e-mail, then using blogging software will be no problem for you.

Some blogging sites offer more features for a fee. Two of these are **SquareSpace** and **Typepad**.

WordPress offers two options — a free, WordPress-hosted blog at **WordPress.com**, or a self-hosted blog at **Wordpress.org**. Self-hosting means that you take the responsibility of finding and paying fees for a server on which to store or "host" your blog.

✳ SELF-HOSTED BLOGS

✳ Why self-host your blog?

For: Freedom and flexibility. You get to use your own domain name, rather than having a blogging provider's name as part of your URL. You have much greater control over the look and feel of your blog. It also allows you to publish your blog free of advertising.

Against: Cost. It's an ongoing expense that will need renewing every year (or two, depending on your choice of host). You might also find you need a bit more expertise to get everything working the way you want it to.

One way to self-host

When you've settled on the domain name you want, go to a hosting company to check for availability. There are lots of companies to choose from, and some offer special packages for bloggers. Enter "compare domain hosting" or something similar in a Web browser to find up-to-date comparisons of domain hosts and the different services they offer. You will usually need access to a credit card, with full permission of the cardholder, to proceed with registering a name.

Once you have your domain name, choose your blogging software. **WordPress** is one of the most popular, and others include **Joomla** and **Drupal**.

If it's available, use the one-click feature from your hosting account to install the software onto the server. There are a number of plug-ins you can add — these are special programs that run on your site. Then simply choose a theme, customize it as much as you like and start blogging.

GET REAL! Teenagers talk about their choice of blog provider

"I use Blogger because most of my favorite blogs use it. I sometimes think that I might convert to WordPress, because it gives a lot more freedom and originality."
(Zoe)

"I use Blogger, but I looked at WordPress too, for blogging on my iPod."
(Reuben)

"I chose Tumblr because I personally think it's easier to use and it's better for teenagers as well, because it's more friendly."
(Megan, who runs http://middletonlove.tumblr.com)

✳ WORDPRESS VS BLOGGER VS TUMBLR

Here's a quick comparison of three of the most popular blog providers.

✳ Blogger

Blogger is owned by **Google** and hosts free blogs with the URL YourBlogName.blogspot.com. Blogger lets you add images and text easily, and it's ideal blogging software for a beginner.
In fact, it's probably best suited to simple blogging using existing templates — more complex customization is not straightforward.
It's also very easy to connect with friends through Blogger. It allows advertising and the use of many third-party widgets — external software programs that can run on your blog.

✳ WordPress

Free **WordPress** blogs have the URL YourBlogName.wordpress.com. WordPress offers a very wide range of free templates and provides thorough instructions for customization. WordPress blogs tend to have a professional, individual look. There are restrictions on advertisements and widgets, so you might find yourself slightly limited in what you can feature on a free WordPress blog.

✳ Tumblr

Tumblr offers free blogs (technically microblogs) with the URL YourBlogName.tumblr.com. Tumblr's templates and features are relatively basic in design, and they are difficult to customize without a knowledge of HTML. The advantage of this is that Tumblr sites tend to have a clean, simplified look. Tumblr is also great for sharing content — users can reblog each other's posts with one click. It's a very friendly, sociable way of blogging.

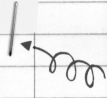

✳ ANATOMY OF A BLOG

Template or theme — The background and basis of design for your blog.

Banner or header — The image and text at the top of the page, giving your blog name, logo and tagline.

Home page — The main page of your blog, and the page that appears when your blog's URL is entered in a browser.

Sidebar — A column on the left or right (or both) of your page's main text.

Other pages — Permanent pages apart from your home page.

Footer — A banner at the bottom of your page, sometimes used to display a copyright notice or link to the tools used in the creation of the blog.

Stands for Completely Automated Public Turing Test to Tell Computers and Humans Apart

✳ SETTING UP YOUR BLOG

Once you've chosen your blogging software, it's simple to set up your blog. Each platform will take you through its own procedure, step by step, but here is a summary of what to expect.

1 Go to the blog provider of your choice. You will be prompted to create a new account, setting a user name and password (if you haven't already done so).

2 You'll be asked to enter the title of your blog. This can usually be changed later, depending on your blogging software.

3 You may be asked to enter a verification code or "**CAPTCHA**" — a code that you copy to prove that you're a human user, rather than a software program trying to create a spam site.

4 You may be asked about other profile settings, such as the kinds of notifications you'd like to receive. These can almost always be altered in the future.

5 You can usually select whether you want your blog to be public (an open site, available to everyone) or private (a closed site, viewable by invitation only).

6 There will be terms and conditions to read and accept.

After this initial input, you'll usually then be prompted to choose a template and begin to design your blog. **Then all that remains is to start blogging!**

✳ BASIC DESIGN TIPS

Try out different templates and features until you find a blog design that you're happy with. Here are some tips that might help:

◎ Choose colors and designs that suit your personality and the theme of your blog.

◎ Make sure that the fonts and color schemes you use aren't difficult to look at. Some color schemes can be unreadable or dazzling — for example, neon text or light text on a dark background. If you want a black background, you could consider using light-colored text boxes on it to avoid this problem.

◎ Think about creating your own top banner or header to go with the color scheme you've chosen.

◎ If you make your own banner, also make yourself a blog button — a smaller version of the image, which other bloggers can copy and use to link back to your blog.

◎ Make your header a clickable link that will take your readers back to your blog's home page. This way, readers of your site will never get lost!

◎ Too many large and moving images might make your blog download slowly and frustrate readers. The same goes for installing too many widgets and plug-ins, such as countdown clocks. On the other hand, using these kinds of programs can liven up your site.

◎ It's a good idea to leave some white space on your page. Blogs can look cluttered without it.

◎ A blog can look cleaner with just one sidebar, but two sidebars give you more space for extra, more permanent information, links and widgets.

Of course, it's up to you to decide what to feature and how to present it. Don't be afraid to experiment!

✳ CUSTOMIZE YOUR BANNER!

Most blogging software will let you make alterations to your blog's basic banner quickly and easily. Still, for a whole new look, you can create a banner that's completely to your taste. There are lots of useful sites around to help you — try searching for "free banner and button maker" to find them. Or look at blogs whose designs you like and see if they credit and link to banner-making software. If not, you could ask the blogger for advice about banner designers. Some designers charge for their services, but others might be fellow bloggers who are happy to exchange links or guest posts for their help.

DIY DUDE

Create your own banner and button

Dude!

You can make an entirely DIY banner with basic graphics software, such as the Paint program that comes with the Microsoft Windows operating system.

Here are step-by-step instructions:

✳ Start with a new document.

✳ Change the size to suit your banner or button.

✳ Use the "fill" tool – the paint can icon – to add color to the background.

✳ Add text using the "text" tool, and paste in any images you require. Experiment with Paint's tools to make changes to the style and positioning of your words and pictures.

✳ Save your banner or button and upload it to your blog.

If you have access to Photoshop editing software, you can make very professional-looking images. An alternative is **GIMP**— freely distributed software for manipulation of images.

http://www.gimp.org

TEST YOUR BLOG

Now that your blog is ready, try creating a few test posts and get the feel of blogging. You can delete them later, together with any sample posts that your blogging platform may have provided for you. Unless you want to start your blog with a retro-looking "Hello World!" post...

ANATOMY OF A BLOG POST

The basic format of a blog post, as supported by all blogging software, is as follows:

Title — The main headline of each post.

Body — The main part of your post, consisting of text, photos and other content.

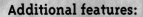

Permalink — The full URL of each blog post, which directs you to the specific blog post rather than to the blog's home page. The permalink often includes the title of the blog post and the date it was posted.

Post date — The date and time stamp showing when the post was published.

Additional features:

Comments — A box where readers can type comments on your post.

Trackback — A notification that another site has linked to your post.

Categories and/or tags — A way to sort posts into groups that you determine, making it easier for users to access other posts on similar topics.

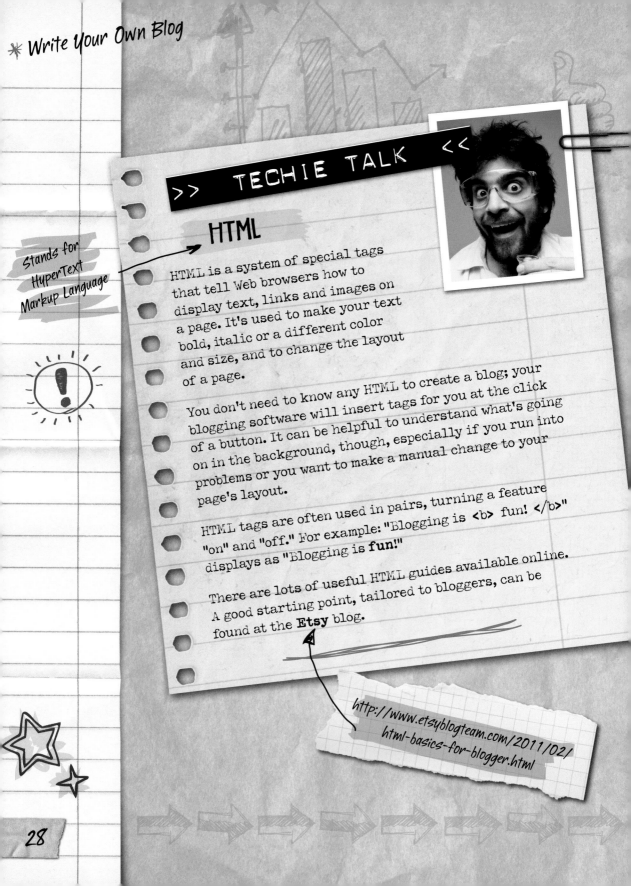

>> TECHIE TALK <<

HTML

Stands for HyperText Markup Language

HTML is a system of special tags that tell Web browsers how to display text, links and images on a page. It's used to make your text bold, italic or a different color and size, and to change the layout of a page.

You don't need to know any HTML to create a blog; your blogging software will insert tags for you at the click of a button. It can be helpful to understand what's going on in the background, though, especially if you run into problems or you want to make a manual change to your page's layout.

HTML tags are often used in pairs, turning a feature "on" and "off." For example: "Blogging is <b> fun! </b>" displays as "Blogging is **fun!**"

There are lots of useful HTML guides available online. A good starting point, tailored to bloggers, can be found at the **Etsy** blog.

http://www.etsyblogteam.com/2011/02/html-basics-for-blogger.html

✳ DIFFERENT WAYS TO BLOG

✳ Bookmarklets

Some blogging software allows you to create a bookmarklet for your browser that you can then use to post to your site. A bookmarklet is a button that displays on your task bar, and acts as a kind of shortcut, ready to perform a series of actions when you click it. It's useful for when you're browsing around and you come across something you want to pop quickly onto your site. **Tumblr** and **Pinterest** are two sites that give you this capability.

✳ Mobile Blogging (moblogging)

Most blogging platforms have special free apps that you can use on your phone for quick and easy mobile blogging.

✳ Posting by E-mail

Most blogging software also allows you to post by e-mail. You need to get hold of a special e-mail address to send your posts to. Check the "help" section of your software for more advice.

QUICK EXPERT SUMMARY

- ◉ Setting up a blog is as easy as using e-mail.

- ◉ You don't need to know HTML to create great-looking pages.

- ◉ You can customize your blog, experiment with styles and features and make the site suit you and your readers.

- ◉ You can usually blog from anywhere with an Internet connection.

Chapter 3

ADDING CONTENT

Now that your blog is up and running, and you've had a chance to experiment with some trial posts, it's time to add some real content.

✳ ADDING PAGES AND POSTS

Decide on any pages you'd like for your blog, and think of some posts you'd like to feature.

Typical pages include "About" and "Contact." You might want to add a privacy policy, or a review policy if it's relevant to your site.

Posts, of course, can be about anything related to the theme of your blog. Many bloggers start with a short post introducing themselves and the site. Diving right in is also fine!

If you write a post and you'd like it to appear at the top of your main page regardless of future updates, you can make it a "featured post" or "sticky post." The term depends on your software, but the result is the same — a post that will always appear first on your home page, until you alter the setting.

✳ WHAT'S THE DIFFERENCE BETWEEN A PAGE AND A POST?

Blog posts are entries that appear in reverse chronological order on your blog's home page. They can be reached through the archives, through tags or categories, and via the RSS feed of your blog. Each post has a URL, or permalink, which usually includes the blog's name and the date and title of the post.

Pages are static, and they don't use tags or categories. They can be listed in a sidebar or tabs at the top or bottom of a blog. Pages have equal status in your blog, and they are not displayed in date order — you can specify the order in which they'll appear on your site. The URL for a page contains your blog's name and the title of the page.

There is no limit to the number of pages or posts you can have in a blog, but too many pages could be hard to access, or could make your blog look cluttered if you make a tab for each one at the top of your page. Large numbers of posts, though, are the whole point of a blog. Make sure that old posts can be accessed easily by adding a "search" feature to your blog and providing links to your archives. You can also add widgets such as **LinkWithin** that offer links to related, older posts under each entry.

 ## USING CATEGORIES AND TAGS

Label your posts with categories and/or tags to group them together into subject areas. This makes it easier for your readers to find what they're interested in, making it more likely that readers will stay on your site and browse your archives.

Some blogging software only allows you to specify categories. If your blogging software allows for tags AND categories, you might be wondering what the difference is.

A category is a broader grouping. Sticking to a small number of categories makes your blog easier to browse. Category names are used in URLs, for example **www.YourBlog.com/Category1** and **www.YourBlog.com/Category2**, and they are often listed in a blog's sidebar for ease of access.

Tags complement your categories and describe your post in more detail. The number of tags you use can be much greater. They don't make up part of a URL, and if displayed in a sidebar they're usually shown in a **cloud.**

This is a *system* that displays the most-used *tags* in a larger font *than* less *frequently* used tags.

For example, in an entertainment blog, "films," "books" and "music" might be categories, and the names of specific directors, authors and singers might be tags.

✳ ADDING IMAGES

You can liven up any blog with images, and all blogging software gives you a simple way to upload images from your computer or phone, or display images from other locations on the Web.

✳ COPYRIGHT ISSUES

It's easy to find pictures for every occasion online, but be aware that using other people's images could be an infringement of copyright law.

Technically, "fair use" of images is sometimes allowed. This means that if you satisfy certain conditions, such as commenting on a picture or using it for research while crediting the owner of the picture, you are allowed limited use. In practice, the law is complicated, and it's safest to avoid relying on fair use as a defense against copyright infringement.

http://www.morguefile.com

http://search.creativecommons.org

A good way around the issue is to use images that are explicitly approved for use by others. There are banks of images, such as **Morguefile**, where you are free to use most images without worrying about copyright, provided you don't claim that the pictures are yours. You can also search using **Creative Commons**, which supports online sharing. Go to the Creative Commons search site and enter what you're looking for to access various image banks. You usually need to give a credit on your site if you use a picture that you've found this way — follow the Creative Commons instructions or find more details in their "Help" pages. Wikimedia Commons is a similar site, and you can also find pictures that are in the public domain and can be freely used. Always check the permissions for each picture.

The process of reblogging means that you display an image or a post from its original location, rather than downloading it to your computer and uploading it to your blog. If someone's post has a "reblog" button on **Tumblr**, for example, this usually means that the blogger will allow you to add his or her content to your own Tumblr, creating an automatic link back to the original post. The same is true of **Pinterest**, a social bookmarking site. When a blogger provides a "pin" button, you can use it to get an "embed" code for use on your site, and this will give automatic credit to the original source.

http://pinterest.com

By far the best way to avoid copyright issues is to build your own bank of photos that you've taken yourself, or illustrations you've drawn and scanned in. You might even want to store these at a site like **Flickr** and list them under Creative Commons for other people's use.

http://flicker.com

✳ AUDIO BLOGS

Audio blogging involves making sound recordings for people to listen to on your site. The term "podcasting" is also sometimes used to mean something very similar.

Audio blogging is straightforward: use some sound-recording software and a microphone to record yourself, and then use your blogging software to post the resulting MP3 file to your blog.

You can get better results if you plan what you're going to say before you start, and you might want to experiment with specialized sound recording software such as **Audacity**, which allows you to spend some time afterwards editing your output. Posting "show notes," or a short description of what you're talking about, can be useful for listeners because they'll be able to see what topics your audio files cover before they listen in.

Groovy!

33

http://www.youtube.com

✳ VLOGS (VIDEO BLOGS)

If you're interested in viewing and making videos, chances are you already have an account on **YouTube**. If not, you'll find that creating this account and building your own video channel is pretty similar to starting a blog. Go to **YouTube**, click on "Sign Up" and follow the instructions. An alternative to YouTube is **Vimeo**, which is often seen as the serious filmmaker's choice of site — the place to be if you're on the arty side.

http://vimeo.com

Make your own videos with your Webcam or phone cam. Look for free video editing software online so that you can experiment with different effects, or just cut out parts you don't like. Then upload your filmic masterpieces to your video channel, where they can be hosted comfortably. From there, it's easy for you to add the videos to your usual blog, letting you combine text and video. Every video on YouTube and Vimeo has an "embed" code, listed under a "Share" or "Add To" tab. All you have to do is find and copy this code, and paste it into the HTML editor of your blog post. Try different size settings if the default doesn't quite fit your blog.

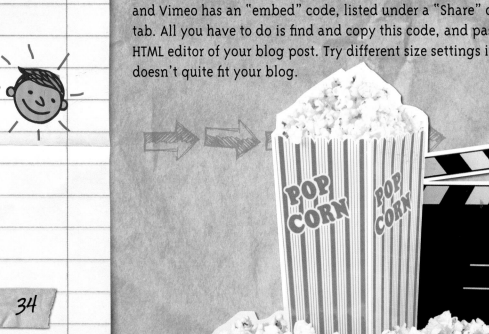

REALITY CHECK

☑ Charlie of charlieissocoollike

Charlie started his vlog in 2007, when he was a teenager who was avoiding studying for his exams. His initial vlogs were broadcast to a small audience, but this grew when one of his videos was featured on the UK YouTube home page. His audience is ever-increasing, and he's now known internationally for his quirky, fun broadcasts.

Maureen Johnson, an author of books for teenagers, is quoted on his Web site as saying: "Charlie is the Internet's second-most important development. The first, of course, is the LOLcat."

Find Charlie at http://www.youtube.com/user/charlieissocoollike, his YouTube channel, and http://charliemcdonnell.com, his Web site.

☑ The VlogBrothers

Popular author John Green and his brother Hank Green run a YouTube channel together known as VlogBrothers. They began by sending messages to each other through regular vlogs in a special project that they called The Brotherhood 2.0. This built up a large audience of dedicated followers, and the Green siblings decided to continue vlogging after the project ended. John Green says of their vlog, "We started making videos at the beginning of 2007... We were able to connect directly with our audience, and it built organically." Find the VlogBrothers YouTube channel at http://www.youtube.com/user/vlogbrothers.

OFFICIAL FORM C-185/A

DIY DUDE

Make some video content and add it to your site

You will need a microphone and a Webcam. It might also be useful to get access to some video editing software. Check online for details of up-to-date software; Windows Live Movie Maker and iMovie are currently both free downloads.

Take some time to prepare what you're going to say. Make some script-like notes and perhaps try a practice run without recording. Then start your Webcam, turn on your microphone and begin.

When you've saved your file, watch it through and edit it if necessary. After that, you'll be ready to upload your file to a site such as **YouTube** or **Vimeo,** which will store it and give you the embed code for displaying it in your blog post. Or you can insert the video directly into your blog if your software supports this. Preview the post and test that everything is working before you publish.

Happy vlogging!

Dude!

✳ MEMES, BLOG HOPS, AND BLOG AWARDS

The word "meme" is usually pronounced to rhyme with "theme." It is a scientific term meaning an idea that spreads from one host to another. The term originated in *The Selfish Gene* by Richard Dawkins as a term for a kind of "idea gene."

In the blogging world, a meme is a type of special feature that's introduced by one blogger and that catches on and spreads among other bloggers. Typical blogging memes include quizzes, questionnaires, surveys and other special types of posts. An example is **Wordless Wednesday**, a popular meme which has been running for years. The idea is that bloggers post a photo — and no text at all — each Wednesday, and they add their link to the Wordless Wednesday site. Around 300 bloggers from all over the world take part in this every week.

http://www.wordlesswednesday.blogspot.co.uk

Many memes will "tag" people. This is an invitation to participate. You list the names of bloggers and sites that you'd like to involve, and send them a message letting them know they have been "tagged" in your meme. Participants in a meme will often leave a link to their blog at the site of the originator, so memes can be a good way to find similar sites and create connections with like-minded bloggers.

Memes can liven up your blog and get you posting if you've been a bit stuck on what to post about. It can also be fun to start your own meme and see whether it catches on.

Another way to find followers, and new blogs to follow, is by taking part in "blog hops." A "blog hop" is also known as a "link-up" or "linky," and it's usually run over a set period of time, such as a day or a weekend. The idea is that you leave a link to your blog — using link-collecting software such as **SimplyLinked** or **Mister Linky** — and then you visit other blogs involved, leaving comments on any that you enjoy. Participants then visit you in return, leaving comments on your site. Look out for blog hops on your favorite sites, or check out sites that list them, such as **Blogaholic Social Network.**

Ahhhh....

http://www.blogaholicnetwork.com

Blog awards are created by bloggers and awarded to blogs they admire, usually following a theme, for example, "Friendly Blogs," "Creative Bloggers" or "Inspirational Posts." The award usually consists of a button or image that you can copy and paste to your blog. Blog awards operate like chain letters — each blog that receives an award is supposed to award it to five blogs in turn, and so on. These types of awards can spread quite far across the blogosphere, depending on the participating bloggers' networks. Some bloggers dislike them, though, or prefer not to take part. It is completely up to you whether to join in with this type of activity. If you'd rather not, it's perfectly fine to thank a blogger for an award and take it no further.

DIY DUDE

Start your own meme

To come up with a meme, consider what you'd like to know about other bloggers, or think of a blog-related subject you'd like to see people discuss. A meme can be as simple as a single question, for example "Which World Record would you most like to break?" Or you could have a dynamic and changing theme, for example, you could call it "Three Thursday Questions" and come up with different questions each week for bloggers to answer on a Thursday.

Once you've decided on your meme, announce it on your blog and be the first to take part. You can make an image button featuring the name of your meme that participants can copy and paste to their sites. Ask other bloggers to leave links to their posts, and tag some blogging friends if you think they would enjoy it. You can use widgets to collect information about participants, such as **SimplyLinked** and **Mister Linky**.

Dude!

QUICK EXPERT SUMMARY

- 🌀 The main body of your blog will consist of posts on the theme of your choice.

- 🌀 You can also add pages, which are static entries such as "About" and "Contact."

- 🌀 Use tags and categories to group similar subjects together and make old posts easier to find.

- 🌀 Liven up your blog with interesting pictures.

- 🌀 You can find images through Creative Commons or reblog them to avoid copyright issues.

- 🌀 Mix things up on your blog by including audio and video content.

- 🌀 Memes, blog hops and blog awards can be a fun way to post and interact with other bloggers.

Chapter 4

KEEP ON BLOGGING

You've started your blog and added some great content. Now you can focus on updating regularly, developing your site and building your readership.

* INSPIRATION FOR BLOG POSTS

Run out of ideas? Can't think of a single thing to post about? Here are a few suggestions that will (hopefully) inspire you.

Make a list. List your favorite books, films, music, food, travel destinations — anything that could make an interesting Top 5 or Top 10.

Your "most wanted." Write about what you wish you could buy if money were no object.

Stuck in the past. If you've been blogging for a long time, think about pulling up a post from the archives and reposting it, giving an update or commentary at the top as you reintroduce it to your readers.

Back to the future. Where do you see yourself in five years' time? What will the world be like then, anyway? Will blogs still exist — and if not, why not? Write about your hopes and dreams for the next few years, and ask your readers about theirs.

Reaction post. Read a few other blogs, especially ones that are outside your usual circle. If you see a post that you feel strongly about, write a reaction to it — either agreeing or disagreeing. Make sure you link back to the original post, and try to express any disagreement in a fair and moderate way. (It might help if you imagine being on the receiving end!)

http://www.thunks.co.uk

Travelogue. Even if you've only been to school or the local shopping center, create a blog version of a road movie as you document your journey. Show pictures of the people and places you've visited and anything interesting you encountered on the way.

Tough one. Ask and answer thought-provoking questions. Have a look at **Thunks** for inspiration, and see if you can come up with your own challenging questions.

What they said. Search for meaningful quotes about topics that you're interested in. There are lots of great quote sites online, for example, **http://www.brainyquote.com.** Post some of your favorite quotes — with attributions — and ask your readers to add their own.

Share the (blog) love. Highlight your favorite blogs, with links, and say why you enjoy them.

✳ TOP TIPS FOR ENGAGING WRITING

After writing blog posts for a while, you might feel like your writing is getting stale. Don't forget: the basic rule is that if you enjoy writing your post, chances are lots of people will enjoy reading it. In case you're worried, though, here are a few hints for writing posts that will keep people hooked:

✳ Your main goal to start with is to get the words down, and to keep going until you've expressed what you wanted to say. At this stage, you're writing a rough draft, so don't worry too much about your spelling or grammar. You'll have lots of time to make changes and corrections before you post, and you can use the spell-check function in your software.

✳ Write as if you're talking to a friend, using your own way of phrasing things. Make your sentences as personal and chatty as you're comfortable with. Don't be afraid to include wordplay and jokes if they come naturally as you write. In short: be yourself!

※ When you've finished, read back over your post a few times, correcting any mistakes you see and making changes to parts you don't like. After that, it's time to think of an interesting headline or title. Come up with something that makes the subject of your post clear. Or, if you go for a more abstract headline, get the subject of your post across in the enticing first sentence of your post.

※ At the end of your post, sum up your argument, or try asking readers for opinions or advice. Then add a couple of eye-catching images, upload your post, sit back and admire your blog!

GET REAL! Something to blog about...

Reuben's focus is more general: "I mainly start my entry with something that happened, and then go on to give a few views on other things to do with it. (e.g. Had a fight with a friend, talk about how petty most arguments are.)"

Amber talks about what she features on her book blog: "If I see something on the Internet about books and I think it would be good to write about it on my blog, then I do. What I blog about often depends on what books I'm sent to review. Also, occasionally my mother will stumble across something on the Internet that she thinks might interest me and will e-mail me the details for me to blog about." Amber runs **The Mile Long Bookshelf** (http://www.themilelongbookshelf.com).

Zoe talks about getting ideas for posts: "If I sometimes think of ideas, I scribble them down in a notebook. I get a lot of inspiration from other blogs but only small ideas of a post, or theme. I don't plan out my posts though, despite having the idea beforehand. I don't like drafting anything, if I am honest!"

✳ SEO: WHAT IS IT AND WHY DOES IT MATTER?

SEO is all about increasing the likelihood that search engines such as **Google** will notice your site and suggest it to people who are searching for the kinds of things you blog about. SEO is measured on two main factors: authority and relevance. The authority is measured by looking at links, especially the number, type and quality of links back to you from other people's sites. The relevance is assessed by analyzing your content — the words and images that you use.

Stands for Search Engine Optimization

The mechanics of SEO can be fairly complex, and some big companies hire staff to concern themselves almost entirely with this side of Web site building. There are pages of information online that will explain the ins and outs of the process; try searching for "Google guide to SEO" for a detailed document. As SEO can help readers to find your blog, it's usually worth at least thinking about a couple of its basic principles.

✳ MAKING YOUR BLOG SEARCHABLE

Text versus images. Generally speaking, text is easier for search engines to scan, especially if it's coded in HTML, which your blogging software will do automatically for you. If your text is hidden within images, it will be difficult for nonhumans to see your content. This matters because search engines send out their robotic data-gatherers to trawl the Web for new sites and material.

Keywords. These are words and phrases that are highly relevant to your post, and the kinds of terms that people might enter in a search engine when they're interested in your post's subject matter. You can identify some good keywords for your post and then make sure that you've used them in your text. For example, if you've written a post containing tips about keeping rabbits as pets, check that your text includes "pet rabbit" and "caring for rabbits." You'll probably find that this occurs naturally and you don't have to give it too much thought.

Headlines and titles. Keywords are even more effective in headlines, so if you run a site featuring author interviews, for example, it's a good idea to use the words "author" and "interview" in your headline. You can also optimize headlines by making sure they are coded correctly with HTML tags.

Meta tags. You can use descriptive "meta tags" on your posts. These are special HTML tags that provide extra information about a Web page, for example, naming the creator of the page and saying what it's about. The information isn't displayed as part of the post, but it comes up in search results and can help users to identify that they've found the right site.

Great content. There's no real substitute for pages of useful and interesting articles, advice and information.

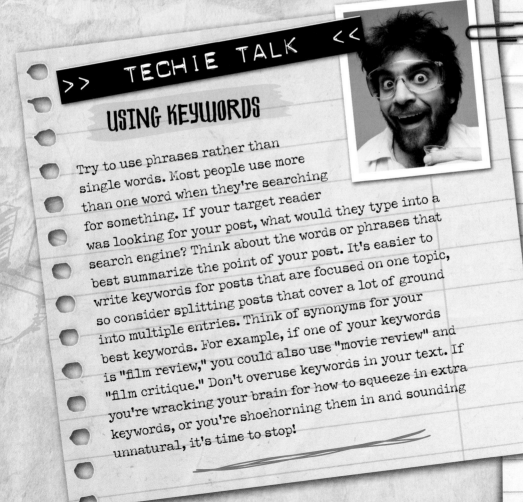

>> TECHIE TALK <<

USING KEYWORDS

Try to use phrases rather than single words. Most people use more than one word when they're searching for something. If your target reader was looking for your post, what would they type into a search engine? Think about the words or phrases that best summarize the point of your post. It's easier to write keywords for posts that are focused on one topic, so consider splitting posts that cover a lot of ground into multiple entries. Think of synonyms for your best keywords. For example, if one of your keywords is "film review," you could also use "movie review" and "film critique." Don't overuse keywords in your text. If you're wracking your brain for how to squeeze in extra keywords, or you're shoehorning them in and sounding unnatural, it's time to stop!

✳ HOW DO YOU KNOW IF ANYONE IS READING YOUR SITE?

Most blogging software provides at least a basic behind-the-scenes capability for calculating the number of times pages and posts on your site have been viewed. These are known as "page views." Sometimes you can also find out the number of "unique visitors," counting visitors to your site only once no matter how many pages they open.

You can usually also look at "referrals" — the sites and searches that are leading readers to your sites. And you can sometimes see the number of people who have subscribed to your feed.

If you would like more information than is available to you through your provider, you can install additional counting tools on your site, many of which are free. Some examples are **Google Analytics**, **SiteMeter** and **StatCounter**. Look out for specialist tools, too, such as one that displays flags to show which countries your visitors are reaching you from. Many sites display simple counter widgets that show the number of times the site has been viewed; these are free to download online or may be available as part of your blogging software.

There are also Web ranking and information companies such as **Alexa.com** and **Compete.com,** where you can register your site to find out how its popularity compares to other sites.

WHAT IS RSS?

RSS is a technology that allows readers to keep track of sites they're interested in. Using RSS, your blog will automatically create what's known as a "feed" or "newsfeed" – an update every time the site's content changes. Readers can click to subscribe to your RSS feed – and you can subscribe to sites you like – in a "feed reader," which is a bit like an e-mail program. New updates will usually show as bold, "unread" posts, and you can organize the sites you're following into different folders. It's a good way to make sure you never miss a single post on your favorite sites.

RSS works with all kinds of blog updates, including audio content in podcasting. Whenever you see the RSS symbol on a site, you can click on it and choose your feed reader from the list, or create a new account, to subscribe.

You can usually create an RSS feed for your blog automatically from your blogging software – search the "Help" pages if necessary. Or you can create an RSS feed from any site using HTML tags – search online for step-by-step advice.

Stands for Really Simple Syndication

QUICK EXPERT SUMMARY

- Keep blog posts fresh and fun by writing them as if you're speaking to your readers.
- Search Engine Optimization (SEO) increases the likelihood that search engines will bring up your site in searches.
- The best thing you can do for SEO is to write good content regularly.
- You can find out how many people are reading your site by looking at stats counters.
- You can gain and keep followers by including an RSS feed link on your site, so that people can subscribe and receive your updates in their feed reader.

Chapter 5

THE SOCIAL SIDE

One huge benefit of blogging is the connections you can make with other people. There are blogging communities of all kinds to find and join. Now that your blog is up and running, your first followers are firmly in place and your readership is increasing, it's time to concentrate on the social side of blogging.

GET REAL!
Social blogging

Zoe from Bookhi says, "My favorite thing about blogging is the people. I love receiving comments. It brightens up my day when I know my posts are liked by people other than myself!"

* TIPS FOR SOCIAL BLOGGING:

- Comment on other blogs and reply to comments on your blog.

- Offer to exchange guest posts with another blogger, or interview each other.

- Think about group blogging, or inviting a regular guest to your site.

- Use **Facebook**, **Twitter** and other relevant social networks to share links to your blog posts.

- Promoting your site through social networks works better when you're engaging with people and posting different kinds of updates too.

WHAT IS SMO?

SMO is a term used to mean "social media optimization." It's also sometimes referred to as "social SEO." Like SEO, it's about improving the reputation of your blog and increasing the number of readers you attract. Instead of being concerned with search engines, the focus is on the social sharing of links to your posts. Features that help with SMO include RSS feeds and post-sharing tools and buttons. Posting links to your blog on social networks also contributes to SMO.

✳ USING SOCIAL NETWORKS TO PROMOTE YOUR BLOG

Create an account on **Twitter** or **Facebook**, or use your existing one, and update your profile with links to your posts and a short, intriguing description. If you have a backlog of posts you want to link to, wait a while between updates so that you don't clutter your friends' timelines with repetitive links.

If you'd rather keep your blog separate from your personal account, make a new account on Twitter using your blog's name. You could use your blog's logo as your profile picture. To promote your blog on Facebook, create a page linked to your account. People can then click "like" and see your blog updates in their timelines.

Most blogging software also provides a way to send automatic updates to your Facebook and Twitter accounts every time you post.

The advantage of this option is that it's quick and easy, and your **Facebook** and **Twitter** followers will never miss out on a post. The disadvantage is that you won't always have full control over the way your update displays, and you might want to add something that is more tailored to your followers on different social networks. Also, the people who read your updates in more than one place will potentially see the exact same text several times.

GET REAL! Teenagers talk about the relevance of Facebook and Twitter to their blogs

"I love social networks. They have exposed a lot of people to my blog. I have a Facebook and Twitter account, both of which are excellent in spreading the word. Even though I prefer Facebook, Twitter has been a lot more successful. I guess that is just because it is more popular – you tweet something and in seconds lots of people have already viewed it. The disadvantage of social networking in my opinion is that it takes a while to set up. You have to gain followers/likes, and eventually it will bring you a lot of benefits." (Zoe)

"I have a Like page on Facebook and a Twitter account for my blog. If I post a link on my Twitter account to my blog, it can get about 50 views in a minute sometimes." (Amber)

✳ EMBEDDING FACEBOOK AND TWITTER WIDGETS ON YOUR SITE

If your blogging software supports widgets and plug-ins, you can show all your **Facebook** and **Twitter** updates in your blog's sidebar. This can keep your site looking lively and active if, for example, you don't post a lot, but you tweet frequently. It can also provide an easy way for your blog's fans to follow you in social networks; they can simply click on the widget to find you.

Find widgets through your blogging software's "Help" pages and follow the installation instructions, or look at the support pages on Twitter and Facebook for advice.

tweet

Note that you can set your Twitter widget to display the tweets of another user, or to follow a Twitter hashtag (a type of keyword). This can be a good way of livening up a fan blog or focusing on a specific subject.

DIY DUDE

Write a social post

Contact a blogger whose site you admire and ask whether you can swap interview questions and be featured on each other's blogs. Decide on questions together, or come up with different sets of questions. Arrange a suitable date for posting, and send questions and answers in plenty of time. Then post on the agreed date, linking back and sending your own readers to the other blogger's site.

Dude!

✳ USING SHARING TOOLS

Another way to get your blog posts noticed is by using online sharing tools. These are provided by sites such as **Google+**, **Digg.com** and **Delicious.com**. Most blogging software allows you to add social sharing buttons at the end of each of your posts, making it easy for users to click through and register their interest. This way they can recommend your post to other readers in their network, spreading the electronic word about your site.

✳ GROUP BLOGGING

A truly social form of blogging is group blogging — running a blog with a few friends or classmates. The blog can be owned by one of you, with others as occasional contributors or guests, or you can have equal status and fully share blog-related tasks. Most blogging software gives you the option of adding contributors who can post directly to your site. The person in charge of the blog administration can restrict the amount of access allowed to others, for example, so that they can post to the blog but not alter the sidebars or layout.

The advantages of group blogging are that you can build a very lively blog with many voices and opinions, and each member of the group will help to spread the word about the site. Disadvantages include needing to consult everyone before making changes, and the potential for disagreements about the running of the site.

Some of the world's most popular blogs are group blogs — **The Huffington Post** is an example, and there are US, UK and Canadian versions of this blog. In the UK, **Girls Heart Books** is a group blog run by authors of books for girls, with each author posting once a month.

http://www.huffingtonpost.com

http://girlsheartbooks.com

Caroline Green, award-winning author of *Dark Ride*, and a contributor to group blog **Strictly Writing** talks about sharing blogging duties:

SAY WHAT?

> The great thing about being part of a shared blog is that when you are feeling low on ideas for subjects to talk about, you have people to discuss it with. Half the time they will help spark an idea. And even if they don't, they feel your pain and don't mind if you have a little moan! It's also lovely to be able to share in the successes of your fellow bloggers.

QUICK EXPERT SUMMARY

- Comment on other people's sites and offer to swap posts and interviews to become part of the blogging community.

- Social Media Optimization is like a social form of SEO and involves the social sharing of links to your posts.

- You can use Twitter and Facebook to promote your blog and post links to your latest posts.

- Give readers the option to use link-sharing tools like Google+ and Delicious after each post, so that they can recommend your post and gain you new followers.

- Group blogging is a sociable way to divide blogging duties.

Chapter 6

AVOIDING BLOGGING PITFALLS AND TROUBLES

Although blogging is fun and rewarding, there can be some minor irritations that cause ripples in the blogosphere. Rarely, there can be more serious trouble. Or you might just find yourself tired of blogging, and wondering whether to keep going with your site. This chapter gives advice for dealing with a few of these issues.

✳ HOW COULD SPAM AFFECT YOUR BLOG?

Spam, spam, spam. It's irritating, but at some point, you're almost guaranteed to see it in the "Comments" section of your blog. You might receive oddly-worded or generic-sounding comments that link back to the spammer's Web site — they'll say things like "Good job!" or "Your blog truly inspires the entire galaxy and beyond." Or you'll get comments that are obviously selling a product or service, usually one that doesn't even have anything to do with your site's subject matter.

The easiest thing to do is to delete spam as soon as you see it. But how can you prevent these nuisance comments from being dumped on your site in the first place?

✳ COMMENT MODERATION AND WORD VERIFICATION

Most blogging software allows you to moderate comments as they come in, which means you can look at them before approving them to appear on your site or rejecting them and marking them as spam. You can also set the "Comments" function to ask users to enter a **CAPTCHA**. These codes prevent spam-bots from blasting fake comments at your site. The downside is that some genuine readers find CAPTCHAs annoying or difficult to use, so you need to weigh the benefits against the potential loss of comments.

Some users turn on comment moderation for older posts only, as this is where the spam often gathers. Blocking anonymous commenters could also cut down on the amount of spam you receive.

✳ OTHER WAYS TO BLOCK SPAM

There is spam-catching software available, for example **Sblam!** and **Akismet**. These services analyze comments from thousands of blogs and block the ones they identify as spam. The process is not completely accurate, though, so you might find yourself needing to scan through the output and making corrections to allow genuine comments to be posted to your site.

Sblam!: http://sblam.com/en.html

Akismet: http://akismet.com

>> TECHIE TALK <<

WHY DO SPAMMERS BOTHER?

The most obvious reason is free advertising. Online advertising is a huge money-making business. Even if most spam comments get deleted, the tiny number that survive can represent an advertising bargain for spammers.

Spam on blogs can have another purpose. When spammers leave hundreds of links with their random comments, they aim to increase their site's search engine ranking. In other words, they're trying to use your site to boost theirs. Block those virtual leeches!

✳ DEALING WITH ONLINE TROLLS AND CYBERBULLIES

Trolls are people who post deliberately annoying or off-topic messages in any online community, including blog comments. They are being disruptive and trying to provoke a negative reaction. Often, the best way to deal with trolls is to ignore them. They're irritating, but they're usually just attention-seekers and will probably go away if they meet a stony silence.

Cyberbullies use Internet technology to intimidate people, harass them and exert power over them. Cyberbullying is much more serious than trolling. If you encounter it, you should always take action. Use your blogging software to block offenders from your site, and tell a trusted adult what has happened. Strongly consider reporting cyberbullies to the authorities.

✳ KEEPING SAFE ONLINE

Check out the site **Think U Know** for detailed advice about staying safe online: **thinkuknow.co.uk/11_16/control** ←

This is run by CEOP, the Child Exploitation and Online Protection Centre.

Some basic guidelines, adapted from **Think U Know**:

 Think before you post, and don't post anything you're unsure about. If you're in any doubt whether you should be posting something, ask a trusted adult his or her opinion. Posts can be deleted, but once something is online it is possible for others to take screen captures of what you've posted.

It's a good idea not to post your full name or the name of your school, and never display your address or phone number.

If anyone makes you feel uncomfortable in the "Comments" section of your blog or in a social network, block them immediately and consider reporting them to your Internet service provider, school authorities, or law enforcement.

Some social media sites also have a built-in system for reporting offensive content. For example, you can click to flag content as inappropriate on each **YouTube** and **Vimeo** video. Search the "Help" section of most social sites to find e-mail addresses for reporting abusive content.

Always speak to a trusted adult if you have any concerns.

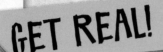

GET REAL! Teenagers talk about dealing with spam, trolls, and cyberbullies

"I did get a few trolls on a blog I co-ran with a friend, and I'm afraid I never looked into it. Let the trolls troll, I guess." (Reuben)

"I had a problem with cyberbullying on my blog a while back. I did overcome it eventually, by blocking the person from my Twitter and Facebook accounts, and also making all comments the person tried to write on my blog automatically go to my spam folder." (Amber)

✳ GETTING INTO TROUBLE FOR BLOGGING

In the past, there have been cases of bloggers getting into trouble for writing about real people and events in an unfavorable way. One of the earliest examples of this was a woman who lost her job after talking about her workplace on her blog, **Dooce.com**. The term "dooced" is still sometimes used to mean "fired for blogging." You can blog anonymously or use an online persona, but even then you should bear in mind that a public blog can be read by absolutely anyone, and someone might be able to identify you. If you post something and regret it, the best way to deal with it is to publish an apology and move on.

✳ BLOGGER'S FATIGUE

Have you started a blog but are already not sure what to post about? Or were you once an enthusiastic blogger whose posts have become irregular to non-existent? Do you find yourself neglecting your blog and feeling guilty? Or are you even starting to resent it a little and wish you'd never started it? You could be suffering from "Blogger's Fatigue"! Don't worry — there are cures.

✳ WAYS TO COMBAT BLOGGER'S FATIGUE

Plan ahead. For example, you can set aside certain days of the week for a particular type of post, such as a meme or a review, so that you have a rough of idea of what you'll be posting in advance. You might find it easier to post if you have a structure to stick to.

Schedule posts. This takes planning one step further. Set posts to go up automatically on certain days, giving yourself some time off from your blog. This is easy to do in the settings of your draft post — select a date in the future before saving and uploading the post.

Don't plan ahead! Do the opposite — post entirely on the spur of the moment about whatever happens to be on your mind. It might give you a new lease on blogging life!

Build a bank. Use any moments when the words are flowing to build up a bank of draft posts that you can adapt for use during very busy times in your life, such as exam time.

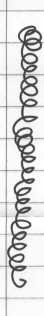

Take a break. Allow yourself a complete rest from blogging if you need it. You might find yourself back and raring to blog sooner than you expect. Before you stop, you could announce on your site that you'll be back shortly, so that readers have an idea of what to expect.

All change! Start a new blog and write about something completely different. After all, it might take you a while to find a style and subject matter that really suit you.

GET REAL! Should you start a new blog?

"I used to have a personal blog, but it went downhill, so I deleted it. However, I didn't want to stop blogging completely because it is so much fun! So I decided to blog about one of my favorite things – books!" (Zoe)

"I started blogging when I left school to be home educated. I used my blog to document the things I was learning at first, and then it became more of a fun thing to do. Since then I've had various blogs, but by far the most successful has been _The Mile Long Bookshelf._" (Amber)

QUICK EXPERT SUMMARY

- Spam consists of unwanted, nuisance messages that are left in the "Comments" section of your blog posts.

- You can use comment moderation and word verification to limit the amount of spam that reaches your blog.

- Trolls are people who deliberately try to annoy bloggers with their comments. They are best ignored.

- Cyberbullies intimidate people online. They should be blocked and reported.

- If you're tired of blogging, change your approach.

THE LAST WORD ON BLOGGING

"I definitely recommend blogging to **everyone**, as it is your space to post what you want. It is your chance to be yourself and **express your opinions** with the world, and **make friends** along the way. I think more kids should blog nowadays too; **I love it**. I nearly always think, "Why didn't I start blogging earlier?" (Zoe)

Build your own book group blog!

Step 1: *Make some plans for your blog*

✳ Once you have formed your blogging group, use blog search engines to look up a few other book blogs and get inspiration and ideas. A good way of finding like-minded blogs is to enter the word "review" plus the title of a book you've recently enjoyed reading.

✳ Discuss what kind of blog you'd like to run. Will you focus on one genre of books (mysteries, comedies, horror, paranormal), or will you have a more general theme? Do you want to include book reviews, author interviews, news about new releases and book covers, or a mixture of these?

✳ Take votes on how to run your blog. Ask yourselves questions like: How often would you like to update your blog? Should there be a rotation for posting, or will things be more informal? Will you have one administrator with overall control, or should everyone have equal access to the blog's inner workings?

Step 2: *Name your site*

✳ Brainstorm together for an appropriate name. Then check with search engines and browsers that the name you want isn't already in use. If it is, find an alternative or adapt it to make it your own.

✳ Think of a tagline that sums up the spirit of your site.

Step 3: *Choose your blogging software*

✳ Look into the pros and cons of different providers before you take the plunge. Which blogging software is used by your favorite book blogs, as identified in Step 1? Sometimes using the same software can help with making connections.

Step 4: *Create an account*

✳ Choose a secure, memorable password, and remember that it can be changed later.

✳ Make sure all the members of your group know what permissions they have to make changes to the blog.

Step 5: *Select a template and design your blog*

✳ Work together to customize the blog features to suit your group.

Step 6: *Add some pages, posts, images and widgets*

✳ Get together to agree on an "About" page describing your interests and what your blog will focus on.

✳ Prepare your first post, introducing your group and stating your goals for the site.

✳ Add relevant links and widgets to your sidebar.

Step 7: *Connect with the blogging community*

✳ Post comments on blogs that share your interests, making sure you link back to your blog. You might want to create a separate e-mail account that's only for use by your group. If so, assign a member or members to check the account regularly.

✳ Post links to your blog posts on social networks.

Step 8: *Keep on blogging*

✳ If inspiration ever fails you, try swapping recommendations. You could challenge a group member who has completely different tastes from you. Try converting them to your favorite genre, and vice versa. Record your mutual success (or failure) on the blog.

Have fun!

blog — A Web site that is regularly updated, with updates displayed in reverse chronological order.

blogger — A person who writes blog posts.

blogging — Writing and updating a blog.

blogosphere — The blogging community.

blogroll — A list of links to other blogs.

CAPTCHA — Stands for Completely Automated Public Turing Test to Tell Computers and Humans Apart.

It is a graphic representation of letters and numbers that a user needs to type to prove he or she is human and not a machine.

categories — Broad descriptions that identify similar posts and group them together.

copyright — The ownership of text or images by the creator.

fair use — The right to use small amounts of copyrighted material for certain purposes.

header — The banner at the top of a site.

HTML — Stands for HyperText Markup Language, and is a programming language used to format Web pages.

keyword — A word or phrase that a person is likely to use in a search engine.

page views — A way of counting the number of times visitors open pages on your blog.

plug-in — A small software program that you install in order to allow your existing software to do something extra.

post — A blog entry.

RSS — Stands for Really Simple Syndication. It is a way of sending blog updates to feed readers.

search engine — A program that suggests relevant Web sites when users enter keywords.

SEO — Stands for Search Engine Optimization. It is a way of making sure your Web site will come up in Web searches.

sidebar — A column on either side of your blog where information can be placed and is permanently visible.

spam — Unwanted comments left on your blog.

tags — Specific keywords that identify similar posts and group them together.

unique visitor count — A way of counting the number of different people who visited your site.

widget — A small software program that you can install from an external source and run on your blog.

>> FOR MORE INFORMATION <<

Fontichiaro, Kristin. *Blog It!* (Information Explorer). Ann Arbor, MI: Cherry Lake Publishing, 2012.

Gardner, Susannah, and Shane Birley. *Blogging for Dummies*. Hoboken, NJ: John Wiley & Sons, Inc., 2012.

Gray, Leon. *What Is a Blog and How Do I Use It?* (Practical Technology). New York, NY: Rosen Publishing, 2014.

Kaplan, Arie. *Blogs: Finding Your Voice, Finding Your Audience* (Digital and Information Literacy). New York, NY: Rosen Central, 2012.

White, Charlie, and John Biggs. *Bloggers Boot Camp: Learning How to Build, Write, and Run a Successful Blog*. Waltham, MA: Focal Press, 2012.

>> WEB SITES <<

Due to the changing nature of Internet links, Rosen Publishing has developed an online list of Web sites related to the subject of this book. This site is updated regularly. Please use this link to access the list:

http://www.rosenlinks.com/QEG/Blog